Featherstone

Series editor
ALISTAIR
BRYCE-CLEGG

fantastic things
to do with **cardboard**

JUDIT HORVATH

Featherstone
An imprint of Bloomsbury Publishing Plc

50 Bedford Square
London
WC1B 3DP
UK

1385 Broadway
New York
NY 10018
USA

www.bloomsbury.com

Bloomsbury is a registered trademark of Bloomsbury Publishing Plc

First published 2017

British Library Cataloguing-in-Publication Data
A catalogue record for this book is available from the British Library.

ISBN:
PB 978-1-4729-2256-4
ePDF 978-1-4729-2478-0

Library of Congress Cataloging-in-Publication Data
A catalogue record for this book is available from the Library of Congress.

10 9 8 7 6 5 4 3 2 1

Printed and bound in India by Replika Press Pvt Ltd.

This book is produced using paper that is made from wood grown in managed, sustainable
forests. It is natural, renewable and recyclable. The logging and manufacturing processes
conform to the environmental regulations of the country of origin.

To view more of our titles please visit www.bloomsbury.com

Contents

Introduction

The main aim of the book

Our children are the future, so teaching them to be keepers of the earth and nature must take priority in their education from as early as possible. When children grow up they will make lifestyle choices based on the familiarity and feeling of positive memories. Using recycled materials during fun and exciting play opportunities will help them understand why and how to use resources in a sustainable way. This collection of *50 Fantastic Things to do with Cardboard* has been collated with the concept of sustainability and low cost in mind. The aim is to provide practitioners with a range of ideas that they can rethink and adapt to their own settings and situations.

Using cardboard boxes can be a combination of reusing and recycling: this book contains simple ideas, as well as more intricate suggestions, all using cardboard, which will be the main resource for making new items, toys or resources. The activities are simple enough for young children to complete with minimal adult guidance; therefore, the projects have the potential to result in genuine sense of achievement for young children.

The structure of the book

The book is based on the seven learning areas of the Early Years Foundation Stage. Each learning area has at least seven activities, providing a varied selection to suit different ages, stages and interests.

Each activity description contains a list of resources required 'What you need'. The activities are clearly explained step-by-step, with easy-to-follow instructions ('What to do'), and suggested extensions and variations for ensuring flexible provision to match different settings, children and individual needs. Additional ideas for similar activities are very helpful when there is a need to take the learning further or to change the direction of the activity. The activities also include some observation questions that offer brief suggestions on how to support the children's learning effectively and to enrich their learning in the future.

The section titled 'What's in it for the children?' describes the educational aims and learning opportunities of the activity. Where needed – due to specific hazards being involved in the flow of the activity – useful information is added in the 'Health & Safety' section; for some activities, adults need to accomplish certain tasks to ensure they are completed safely, e.g. handling sharp tools to cut hard fruit. Practitioners should make informed decisions about which tasks can be safely accomplished by which of their children, and always adhere to the Health & Safety procedures in place within their setting.

Learning with cardboard boxes

For young children the world around them is full of interesting materials to touch, discover, explore, collect, sort and use. Open-ended play materials all have unique, yet very flexible characteristics, and exploring them gives the children both motivation and inspiration for discovering and learning in individual ways. This type of learning is usually an evocative experience for the children: it stimulates the imagination and invites them to create stories, act out situations and play games. Cardboard boxes can engage children for hours on end with minimal cost and impact on the environment. But more than that, playing with a cardboard box can build skills that toys with more parts and colours cannot necessarily develop: creativity, imagination and resourcefulness. Cardboard boxes spark the imagination as the children build upon, transform and reinvent them. The cardboard box takes them on adventures and helps them explore imaginary places in their minds.

The best kind of play with boxes is unstructured play, which gives children the opportunity to explore versatile open-ended materials without an end result in mind, whilst also aiding many areas of development. However, the 50 activities in this book will act as brilliant inspirational starting points. Tools and real objects as opposed to the toy versions are fascinating for young children, and should be incorporated into their daily lives so they get used to taking small risks in a safe place.

The best boxes...

Many shops will be willing to donate unwanted boxes and packaging to your setting. Invite parents to donate others from home too. When carrying out the projects, some activities will need a certain type of cardboard (soft, corrugated etc.), but the majority can be completed with any type of box or used cardboard packaging.

Building with cardboard boxes
Physical development

What you need:

- **Cardboard boxes in various sizes** (cereal boxes, nappy boxes, toy boxes)
- **Cardboard tubes** (kitchen roll and toilet roll inners)
- **Photographs of buildings, arches and bridges from magazines/internet**
- **Builders' hats**
- **A large space to build**

What to do:

1. Collect cardboard boxes in different shapes and sizes. The more interesting the boxes collected, the wider the variety of buildings the children can construct.
2. Lay the boxes out in a large space.
3. Provide photographs of buildings to give the children inspiration.
4. Supply builders' hats and leave these scattered around the boxes.
5. Encourage the children to become builders and make their own construction using the boxes. If they struggle, provide an example of a cardboard building that you made yourself.

Taking it forward

- The activity can be adapted to suit different age groups based on the size of the boxes provided. If using smaller boxes, add pipe cleaners and sticky tape to make connections. If using larger ones, provide rope and black and yellow hazard tape.

- Provide scarves, larger pieces of fabric and torches so the children can create sensory dens/caves with the boxes.

Observation questions

- What size of material can the child efficiently use?

- How does the child control their own body in the given space with the provided materials?

What's in it for the children?

Apart from using gross motor skills and taking part in a fun exercise, children will also learn about different sizes, shapes and weights whilst understanding the basic concept of balance.

Make a train

What you need:

- Large cardboard boxes
- Strong string or thin rope
- Sticky tape
- Newspaper
- Felt tip pens
- A large space to build
- Castor wheels, nuts and bolts (optional)
- Old long scarf (optional)

What to do:

1. Collect large cardboard boxes.

2. Ask children to design a train and help them to cut off the top of the boxes and to create windows and doors on the sides.

3. Create holes at the ends of the cardboard box carriages and connect them with the string.

4. Cut circles from the unused box tops to make the wheels.

5. Optionally, add castor wheels and secure them with nuts and bolts, so the train can be moved.

6. Use felt tip pens to decorate the train. As a final feature, you could attach an old scarf to create a pull strap.

7. Cut long strips of newspaper and connect with sticky tape to create the rail tracks.

Taking it forward

- By providing sticks, paper, pens, torches (to act as a train signal) the activity can become a train station role play.

- Children's large muscle groups can be activated by providing different materials to load the trains and children can pull/push the carriages.

Observation questions

- What are the child's body movements like?

- Are their movements jerky, uncertain or poorly coordinated?

What's in it for the children?

As well as exercising by lifting boxes and climbing in and out, children will also learn about different sizes, shapes, and weights whilst understanding the basic concept of balance and making connections.

Pirate ship
Physical development

What you need:

- One large cardboard box
- Sticks and branches in various sizes
- Light fabric pieces such as old scarves
- String
- Sticky tape

What to do:

1. Collect the materials with the children.

2. Cut the top off the boxes to create the ship.

3. Create holes in the ends of the box and attach the masts made out of sticks and branches with string and/or sticky tape.

4. Tie on the fabric sail.

5. Enjoy the pirate ship role play together.

Taking it forward

- Provide smaller cardboard tubes to create telescopes to use on the ship.
- By making more than one pirate ship, the children can take part in simple games and team competitions.
- Provide food and organise a pirate themed tea party where you can encourage the children to try new, unusual tastes such as seafood.

Observational questions

- Is the child showing increasing fine motor control when using tools?
- Can the child efficiently move in and out of the space provided?

What's in it for the children?

Children can learn about their own bodies and how exercise affects them whilst exploring the ship.

Marionette

Physical development

What you need:

- **Small, thin cardboard boxes** (cereal box)
- **Scissors**
- **Markers, crayons**
- **Pieces of fabric** (old T-shirt cut up)
- **Pieces of newspaper**
- **Brass fasteners**
- **Sticks or pencils**
- **Cotton or fishing line**
- **Needle**
- **School glue**

Taking it forward

- Organise a marionette puppet show.
- Make animal marionettes to compare human and animal bodies.

Observational questions

- How does the child incorporate movement into their communication?
- How does the child perform the movements?
- How is fine motor control developing?

What's in it for the children?

Children can learn about their body parts. They can observe how the body parts are connected, how the body moves and what the effects of physical exercise are.

What to do:

1. Collect small boxes, thin enough for children to cut shapes out of.

2. Explain to the children that they are going to design a moving puppet and decorate it with markers, crayons, newspaper or fabric pieces.

3. Lay out the puppet: assemble it face-up on a flat surface. Cut and lay out a torso-shaped piece first, then cut out and arrange pieces of cardboard for the arms and legs so that a section of each overlaps with the torso piece.

4. Create the joints by pushing a brass fastener through each joint in the puppet (punch holes in the card if it is too thick to be pierced by the fastener alone). The joints should remain loose and flexible enough for the limbs to move easily.

5. Create the handle by laying down two pieces of a stick or pencils to form a cross. Tape the sticks together where they intersect.

6. Attach the strings to the body: thread a needle with cotton, or fishing line if you want the strings to be transparent, then pierce a hole through the cardboard just above the knees and the wrists. Pull the thread through, then knot it and cut off the excess after making each attachment. The length of the puppet string extending from each section needs to be long enough to reach the sticks, which should be at least 15cm above the shoulders.

7. Tie the strings extending from the puppet's shoulders to the centre of the cross. Knot each of the four strings connected to the puppet's limbs to an individual arm of the cross. Dot glue on each knot to keep it from untying.

What you need:

- Cardboard boxes in different sizes
- Ribbons
- Scissors
- Lengths of string

What to do:

1. Collect the materials with the children.

2. Show the children how to make different types of connections to join the boxes to each other.

3. Create holes in the boxes and attach ribbon and string pieces to create connections and attach different boxes together.

4. Move the connected creation and see which fixings are the strongest.

Taking it forward

With the children, research connections in the human world such as bridges and walkways, and try to copy them.

Observation question

How does the child use the physical space in relation to size and shape of self and objects?

What's in it for the children?

Children can gain knowledge about how materials and objects connect and how things relate (with regards to their shape or size) which they can use in their own construction attempts.

50 fantastic things to do with cardboard

Let's make a den

Physical development

What you need:

- **Large cardboard box**
- **Different pieces of fabric** (old sheets or blankets, scarves)
- **Lengths of string**
- **Paper and pencils**

What to do:

1. Collect the materials with the children.
2. Talk about what a den is and plan one together with the children, creating sketches.
3. Cut the top flaps off the box and turn it on its side.
4. Make holes in the top of the box.
5. Take the fabric and gather the corners. Tie string around the bundled material, then thread through the holes in the boxes to secure and enclose the den.
6. Allow children to use the den in small groups.

Observational questions

- Does the child manipulate their body well?
- Does the child notice changes in the body in relation to the activity?

What's in it for the children?

Children can create their own safe place and learn about their own body by being in a social group close together.

Taking it forward

- Fix fairy lights inside to create a magical den and play with shadows to learn how the reflections of different people and different body parts vary.
- Add small pieces of furniture inside to make a home – let the children practise how to make their bodies smaller or larger.
- Collect torches and shiny objects to make a sensory den for a relaxing effect on the body and eyes.

Cardboard furniture

Physical development

What you need:

- Large, serrated cardboard boxes
- Strong scissors
- Markers, felt tip pens
- PVA glue
- Pillows
- Long, straight sticks
- Fabric pieces

What to do:

1. Collect large boxes.

2. Design pieces of furniture with the children.

3. To make a bed: use a long, shallow box, cut the top flaps off and place pillows inside.

4. To make a wardrobe: stand a rectangular box up, cut the smaller flaps off and leave long flaps to act as doors.

5. To make a cupboard: use a smaller rectangular box and stand it on its side. Cut the smaller flaps off, and use the larger flaps as the cupboard doors. You could also keep one of the smaller flaps to make a shelf inside the cupboard. First, measure and draw a line inside the box at the height at which you would like the shelf to sit. Then, mark out two evenly spaced points along the line on both sides of the box; these will be used a holes for the shelf supports. Push long, straight sticks through each hole and rest your 'flap shelf' on top.

6. Children can colour, paint or cover their furniture with fabric.

Taking it forward

Make a furniture shop.

Observational questions

Does the child show patterns of behaviour/movement when playing?

Does the child follow certain schemas?

What's in it for the children?

Children can learn to experience how to negotiate space for themselves when working with objects or when being with others.

Giant robot

Physical development

What you need:

- Large cardboard boxes
- Long cardboard tubes (for limbs)
- Empty cans
- Paper and plastic cups
- Markers, felt tip pens
- Aluminium foil
- Used CDs
- Sticky tape
- PVA glue
- String

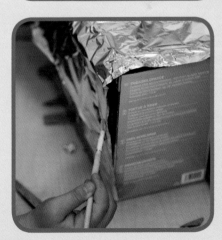

What to do:

1. Collect large boxes.

2. With the children, design a robot based on pictures that you have collected and printed off from an internet search or by looking through related books together.

3. Start by covering the boxes with aluminium foil pieces, wrapping them well around the sections.

4. Construct the robot following the children's design, connecting pieces with glue or string.

5. Attach the robot to a broom handle or large branch so that it is supported and can be displayed for further use.

Taking it forward

- Have fun moving and talking like robots.
- Make a robot head from a box for children to wear.
- Talk about outer space experiences: what happens to the body in space?
- Make smaller robots for children to personalise, take home and look after.
- Create a story about the adventures of the robot.

Observational questions

- How interested is the child in what he/she is doing?
- Does he/she seem intent on what he/she is doing or does the child seem more interested in what others are doing?
- How long is she/he able to concentrate?

What's in it for the children?

Children can learn about their body and its physical characteristics, weight and height.

Box of memories
Personal, social and emotional development

What you need:

- **Cardboard boxes in various sizes** (cereal boxes, nappy boxes, toy boxes)

Materials to decorate:

- **natural materials:** leaves, berries, sticks, grass, flowers, petals, sand
- **covering materials:** glue, sticky tape, paper, fabric, foil, glitter
- **drawing/painting:** pens, pencils, crayons, paint

What to do:

1. Collect cardboard boxes in different shapes and sizes. The more interesting the boxes collected, the more different styles the children can choose from.

2. Allow each child to choose a box and offer them a selection of different media to decorate their box in their own style.

3. Ask the children whether they would like their box open or 'secret' when displayed and display them accordingly

4. Encourage children to store/place their personal objects in their boxes.

5. Ask children whether they would like to present the content of their boxes to the other children in circle time.

Taking it forward

- Children can create a box for their families to communicate what they find important within their family relationships.

- Children can express their views of others by making personalised boxes for their friends or family.

Observational questions

- How easily does the child make decisions?

- What important things does the child keep in their box?

What's in it for the children?

Children can store their personal collection of important objects in their boxes to ensure their sense of safety and security. They can experience the feeling of responsibility when making choices and looking after their own box.

A treasure chest

Personal, social and emotional development

What you need:

- Cardboard boxes in various sizes
- Map of the local area
- Materials to decorate
- PVA glue
- Duct tape
- Scissors

What to do:

1. Collect cardboard boxes in different shapes and sizes.
2. Flatten the larger cardboard boxes to create a large surface for children to draw on.
3. Ask the children to recall familiar places using a real map of the area where they live.
4. Using the map, help the children to create their own treasure island map of their home town on the large flattened surface, showing the personal route they take to nursery, to the shops or to their grandparents.
5. Ask the children to collect objects, something to connect with each significant place, e.g. nursery, school, park, shop etc.
6. Personalise smaller boxes with decoration chosen by the children and collect gathered items in the personal treasure box.
7. Follow the personal map of each child and use the treasure boxes to share stories and talk about personal objects.

Taking it forward

Children can record the story of their journey to nursery for others to listen to.

Observational questions

How does the child feel about what he/she is doing? Does the child seem happy? Upset? Satisfied?

Does he/she ask for help or seem to need encouragement?

Does he/she try new things on his/her own or wait for coaxing?

What's in it for the children?

Children can learn to express their views whilst also developing their memory. They can develop listening and empathy skills whilst appreciating the notion of personal belongings.

50 fantastic things to do with cardboard

Doll's house and furniture

Personal, social and emotional development

What you need:

- Cardboard boxes in various sizes
- Plastic or paper straws
- Sticks, branches, pencils
- Leaves
- Paper pieces to decorate
- Coloured foam
- PVA glue
- Duct tape
- Scissors
- Beads
- Small wires

What to do:

1. Collect cardboard boxes in different shapes and sizes.

2. To create a doll's house, simply cut the flaps/top off a larger box and turn it on its side.

3. To make a bed: use a cereal box. Cover four pencils or small sticks with duct tape – these will be the bed legs. Using extra cardboard, cut out a headboard and footboard, then cover them in duct tape. Create a mattress by using another cereal box, cutting out one of the large sides and then filling the box with stuffing before covering it in fabric. Stuff the last side with mattress stuffing, then cover with duct tape. Attach the headboard and footboard with duct tape to the bedframe box, then attach the pencils with duct tape to each corner for legs. Add a piece of fabric for a blanket, and pillows.

4. To make a table: cut out and paint a circle of cardboard. Once dry, cut out four pieces of straw and secure onto the circle. If using bendy straws, take four of them and include the concertina-like section at the top of each, so that for each table leg you can bend it at right-angles and tape onto the underside of the cardboard circle. Glue two of the pieces towards the front and two towards the back, placed evenly from the edge.

5. To make a bath tub: paint a small box white. When dry use coloured paper to cut out a frame for around the top of the tub and glue on. Then cut foam into squares and glue them all around the box to create a tile effect. Bend a small piece of wire for a tap, make a small hole in the box and secure in place with glue. Glue your beads on for the hot and cold handles.

6. Everyday objects like bottle tops can be used to make a sink or rubbish bin.

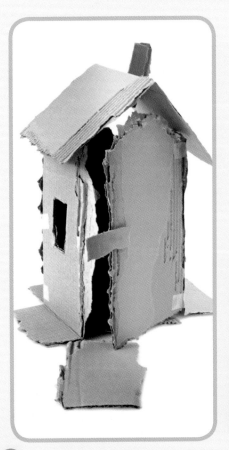

18

Children bring in pictures of their own homes to copy.

Children can create a story of a stick family to act out.

bservational questions

Does the child talk about their own family?

Does the child share personal experiences?

'hat's in it for the children?

hildren can express the views of their wn family when playing with a family of olls in the doll's house. They can also hare stories and listen to others as they ay.

Mood faces
Personal, social and emotional development

What you need:

- Printable face mask templates
- **Thin cardboard boxes** (tissue, cereal etc.)
- Mirrors
- Scissors
- Pencil
- Glue
- Hole punch
- Ribbon
- Paint

What to do:

1. Collect thin cardboard boxes in different shapes and sizes and cut them up to create large flat pieces.
2. Look at printed face mask templates on the internet together and talk about making your own masks.
3. Invite children to sketch a mask whilst observing their own faces in the mirror.
4. Use scissors to cut the shapes out of the cardboard and use paints to decorate the masks.
5. Punch one hole on each side of the mask, and secure a length of ribbon to each side for tying.
6. Use the mask in circle time to discuss feelings.

Taking it forward

- Children can use the masks to match the feelings of characters in classic stories.
- Children can look at photographs of people in newspapers and magazines and discuss what people may be feeling.

Observational questions

- Does the child show empathy?
- Can the child verbally or facially express a feeling?

What's in it for the children?

Children can learn to express their feelings and learn to appreciate the feelings of others. They can also study the physical signs of different feelings (facial expression, posture etc.).

Cardboard city

Personal, social and emotional development

What you need:

- Empty matchboxes and other small boxes
- Small cardboard boxes
- Scissors
- Ruler
- Pencil, marker pen
- Glue
- Duct tape
- Paint

What to do:

1. Collect and organise all of the materials.

2. To create a building: use a ruler and pencil or marker pen to draw and create an outline of each side of the building, complete with window, door and decoration markings. Cut the outlines and place each building's sides and other pieces in separate piles to organise each project individually. Line up the pieces of buildings in an upright fashion to check each side is equal to one another and has an even edge for gluing or taping. Tape or glue the sides together, using duct or masking tape and sealing each side of the building with craft or instant super glue.

3. Allow the building to dry before attempting to decorate the structure. Add a roof to a building by cutting out an additional piece of cardboard to fit snugly over the top of the structure, or create the shape of a cone or triangle. Secure the roof to the top of the structure by using tape and glue. Paint or decorate the building. Choose different colours for doors and windows to add contrast and life to the city made up of all the different buildings.

4. Use thin card or coloured paper to create patches of grass, carpet or other street decorations in the city.

5. To assemble: use a large piece of flat cardboard as a base to draw streets and roads on, then glue on the houses/buildings.

Taking it forward

Children can bring in photographs of their own homes to copy.

Study different forms of living around the world (tribal living, big cities, small villages) and make different style cardboard cities.

Add cars, trees, traffic lights etc.

Observational questions

How does the child get along with other children?

Does he/she play alone, with only certain children, or with a variety of children?

Does he/she initiate or follow along with group ideas?

What's in it for the children?

Children can learn about where people live, sharing their experiences about different forms of living.

50 fantastic things to do with cardboard

The pet keeper's box

Personal, social and emotional development

What you need:

- Small boxes
- Selection of soft toy animals
- Scissors
- Pencil, marker
- Decoration materials
- Glue, tape
- Paint

What to do:

1. Collect cardboard boxes (about A4 size).

2. Choose the pet (soft toy animal).

3. Decorate box/boxes with appropriate drawings, pictures and materials. For example a dog-keeper's box can be covered in furry material and bone shapes.

4. Provide a collection of objects that the children think is essential for looking after each pet, such as a bowl to drink from, a brush, bone, gloves, blanket etc.

5. Designate a keeper for each day.

Taking it forward

- Children can make a box themed on a pet they have at home, or a friend or neighbour's pet.

- Organise a veterinary service in your role play area.

Observational questions

- How does the child behave when being responsible for the box? Cooperative? Bossy?

- Does the child show interest/ empathy towards animals?

What's in it for the children?

Children can learn about responsibility. They can experience the feeling of 'being in charge' and being the decision-maker. Children will learn about cause and effect whilst also developing reasoning skills.

Picnic basket
Personal, social and emotional development

What you need:

- Tape or glue
- Scissors
- Stapler
- Stickers
- Ribbon
- Silk or real flowers
- Juice or milk carton
- Coloured paper

What to do:

1. Rinse out and dry a juice or milk carton or use a larger cardboard box.

2. Cut out the side that has the spout.

3. Take a piece of coloured paper and measure it against the carton, tracing out each side. Then cover each side with the coloured paper, using either tape or glue.

4. Take another piece of coloured paper and cut out a long piece about 5cm wide for the handle. Staple it to the carton.

5. Children can use flowers or stickers to cover the staple and to decorate the basket.

6. Put picnic items in the basket and use it as a part of a role play or real picnic.

Taking it forward

- Children can make their own food to keep in the picnic box.

Observational questions

- Does the child make decisions easily?

- Is the child influenced by their surroundings?

What's in it for the children?

Children can learn about responsibility, looking after their own food for the picnic. They can gain a sense of ownership by possessing their own basket and also respecting that of others.

Market stall

Communication and language

What you need:

- Serrated cardboard boxes, large and shallow
- Scissors
- Play or real vegetables
- String

What to do:

1. Collect cardboard boxes in different shapes and sizes.
2. To make the base of the market stall, stand a large box upright and pierce four holes in the top (originally the side) in the shape of a rectangle.
3. To make the container, cut off the flaps of a shallow box, and place it on top of the base. Pierce holes on the shallow box in line with the ones pierced on the base, and lead two pieces of string through both sets of holes, to secure the shallow box on top. Then, tape the string down to each box to strengthen the ties. Children can paint their stalls brown to create a wooden effect.
4. Use real vegetables to encourage a market stall role play.

Taking it forward

- Children can grow/bring in and sell/exchange their own vegetables.
- Secure two broom handles to the stall, one on either side, then cut out and attach a large piece of cardboard to the tops of the broom handles and paint it in stripes to create typical market stall roofing.
- Children can make their own paper money for the role play.

Observation questions

- How does the child negotiate?
- What is the child's vocabulary like?

What's in it for the children?

The role play will encourage children to communicate and socialise with their peers. Less confident children can be given special roles to encourage them to take part, in order to learn to negotiate via clear communication.

What you need:

- **Cardboard boxes in various sizes** (cereal boxes, nappy boxes, toy boxes)
- **Cardboard tubes**
- **Materials to decorate**
- **Glue**
- **Tape**
- **Aluminium foil**

What to do:

1. Collect cardboard boxes in different shapes and sizes to make the story collection boxes.

2. To make a castle: cut the flaps off the box and cover the box with aluminium foil. Cover four cardboard tubes with aluminium foil (these will form your turrets), then cut four circles out of a piece of any kind of paper. The height of turret will be determined by the radius of circle. Cut out a triangle/wedge/section by making two cuts to paper or card, then cut a line from the edge into the middle of each circle. Fold the paper circles round on themselves to create cones. Attach each cone to the top of the cardboard tubes, then finally secure the turrets onto the four corners of the box.

3. To make a boat: draw out the basic shape of the bottom of the boat and cut out. Create the sides by cutting cardboard strips to match the perimeter of the boat. Line up the sides to the base. Tape the sides on to the base and then tape together.

4. The children can take their story castles/boats home and collect objects to store in them. They can bring them back into the setting to talk about the contents and why the objects they have collected are important to them.

Taking it forward

- Children can design their own boxes, according to their interests.
- Create a gallery and exhibit the creations.

Observational questions

- How easily does the child make decisions?
- What does the child find to keep in their story box?

What's in it for the children?

The collection of objects will help the children to recall events and feelings, and aid them in communicating their thoughts to their peers, responding to the world around them.

Word dice

Communication and language

What you need:

- Square tissue box or other thin cardboard box
- Glue
- Plain paper to cover the box
- White cardboard or paper
- Scissors
- Marker pens

What to do:

1. If you are using a square tissue box, cover all the sides with glue and plain paper.

2. Use a template (like the one below) for making a cube to cut out a matching cardboard shape. Fold the cube into shape and use the tabs to glue the box together.

3. Write the names of everyday objects on the sides of dice in different languages and stick a picture on to aid understanding.

4. The dice can be used in circle time to encourage children to listen to words in different languages.

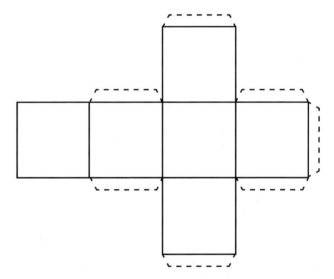

Taking it forward

- Children can create their own dice to take home. This is really helpful for children with English as a second language.
- Listen to text in different languages with the children and try to recognise foreign words.
- Use a map to match languages and countries.

Observational questions

- Do children show an interest in different languages?
- Can children remember words?
- Can the child recognise patterns/ sounds?

What's in it for the children?

Listening to words in different languages will help children to understand the meaning of print as they compare the look of words. It will help children to develop appreciation of other cultures.

The monster box
Communication and language

What you need:

- **Tissue box**
- **Glue**
- **Plain paper**
- **Sticky tape**
- **White cardboard or paper**
- **Scissors**
- **Decorations** (coloured paper spots, wool, egg cartons)

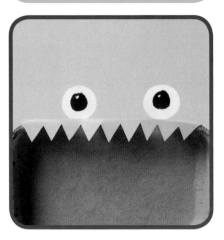

What to do:

1. Remove the plastic insert from the inside of the tissue box opening.
2. Wrap the box in paper with the opening face down so the sticky tape areas are to the back.
3. Using scissors, cut a hole into the opening through the paper.
4. Create teeth by cutting strips of paper or cardboard with jagged edges and attach these to the opening.
5. Children can decorate their monster with coloured paper spots or stickers, wool for hair, pipe cleaner arms or antennas and egg carton eyes.
6. Organise a 'space journey' in the garden/park and encourage the children to take their monster on an adventure.

Taking it forward

- Create characters of classic fairy tales and go on a journey in the woods.

Observation questions

- Does the child ask questions?
- Can the child pronounce new words?

What's in it for the children?

Using specific words when talking about a theme (such as space) will aid children in developing a wider vocabulary and in the understanding of the meaning of words. Children will develop a more advanced understanding of the connection between objects, words and meaning.

Rhyme and song dice

Communication and language

What you need:

- Square tissue box or other thin cardboard box
- Glue
- Plain paper
- White cardboard or paper
- Scissors
- Pictures to represent nursery rhymes or the children's favourite songs

What to do:

1. If using a square tissue box, cover the sides with glue and stick on plain paper.

2. Use a template (like the one below) for making a cube to cut out a matching cardboard shape. Fold the cube into shape and use the tabs to glue the box together.

3. Draw or stick pictures on all sides of the dice relating to nursery rhymes or children's favourite songs.

4. The dice can be used at circle time to encourage children to sing, to remember rhymes or to learn new songs.

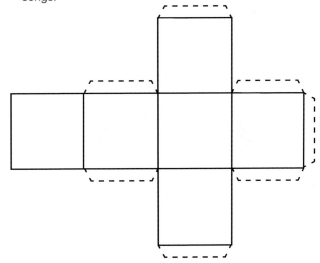

Taking it forward

- Children can create their own dice to take home.

- Children can use instruments, and pictures of instruments on the dice, to encourage the use of rhythm.

Observation questions

- Does the child know nursery rhymes?

- Can the child connect picture to rhyme?

What's in it for the children?

Rhyming will help children's memory and identification skills. Connecting pictures to rhymes will support children in the understanding of print, writing and reading.

Pebble faces
Communication and language

What you need:

- Mirror
- Pebbles
- Seashells
- Seaweed
- Coral pieces
- Sticks
- Glue
- Tape
- String
- White cardboard or paper
- Scissors

What to do:

1. Ideally, select larger pebbles that have face or body shapes. However, any pebble can become a face or a body with some imagination!

2. Ask the children to look at their own reflection in mirrors and then create a face on their chosen pebble with nose, eyes, mouth and ears.

3. Use all types of seashells, seaweed and pieces of coral for hair, ears, eyes, noses and mouths or create them with a black marker pen.

4. Draw a body on a piece of cardboard, cut it out and stick the pebble face on.

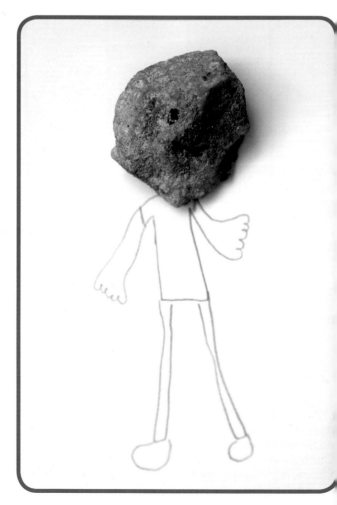

Taking it forward

- Children can create pebble characters from stories.

- Children can create their own pebble family, trying to copy the characteristics of their family members.

Observation questions

- Can the child follow simple instructions?

What's in it for the children?

Children will learn to understand simple instructions when making the pebble people.

Leaf puppets

Mathematics

What you need:

- Cardboard tubes
- Pebbles or bark
- Leaves
- Twigs
- Wiggley eyes

What to do:

1. Begin by gluing the leaf to the top of the cardboard tube for the head.

2. Glue the twigs to the sides of the tube for the arms or pierce a hole and secure the arms in the hole.

3. Glue pebbles or small pieces of bark to the front of the tube for buttons.

4. Add wiggley eyes to the leaf head.

5. Invite the children to vocalise the 'thoughts' of their puppet.

aking it forward

Children can use puppets to create their own theatre and act out favourite stories (such as *Stick man* by Julia Donaldson).

Children can create their own puppet family, trying to copy the characteristics of their family members.

bservation questions

Can the child mimic?

Can the child use and understand different tones of voice?

'hat's in it for the children?

hildren experiment with their
wn voices, creating sounds and
odelling language. This will support
hildren's ability to communicate and
nderstand non-verbal communication
ke tone of voice.

Sorter boxes
Mathematics

What you need:

- Shells
- Pebbles
- Leaves
- Sticks
- Buttons
- Coins
- Feathers
- Conkers
- Small cardboard boxes
- Egg cartons

What to do:

1. Cut the top off several small boxes and tape them together or cut up egg cartons into individual sections.

2. Give children a selection of small items to sort into the small boxes. Talk about the similarities and differences of objects (weight, size, colour, texture etc.). Let the children decide the criteria for sorting items.

Taking it forward

- Organise a competition by timing the sorting individually and in groups.

- Once sorted, create pictures of the collections by sticking them on pieces of flat cardboard.

Observation questions

- Can the child recognise patterns?

- What vocabulary does the child use to describe and sort objects?

What's in it for the children?

Children will develop an understanding of similarities, differences and patterns.

Mathematics

What you need:

- A selection of cardboard boxes in different sizes
- A selection of large and small objects

What to do:

1. Encourage the children to rank the boxes based on size. Use mathematical vocabulary such as tall/ taller, wide/ wider etc.

2. Line up the boxes, small to large or large to small.

3. Place objects into the boxes.

4. Talk about similarities and differences of objects (weight, size, colour, texture etc.).

aking it forward

Stack boxes in size order to create towers.

bservation questions

Does the child realise the differences in size?

Does the child use mathematical language to describe size?

hat's in it for the children?

hildren will develop an understanding f qualities and quantities.

Giant dice
Mathematics

What you need:

- **A very large square box** (as big as the children)
- **Parcel tape**
- **Paint**
- **Newspaper**
- **Scissors**
- **Glue**

What to do:

1. Take a large box and tape the joins on the box to strengthen it.

2. Paint the box all over.

3. Once dry, use the newpaper to cut out large numerals and stick a number on each side of the box.

4. Use your giant dice in games such as throwing the dice then asking children to copy the number it lands on or collect that number of objects from around the setting o outdoor area.

Taking it forward

- Use the giant dice in board games for fun.

- In activities, use the giant dice to encourage exercise, for example 'hop as many time as the number on the dice'.

Observation questions

- Can the child count by rote?

What's in it for the children?

Children will develop an understanding that things can be counted, whilst associating number of objects with numerals.

Shapes and shape sorter

Mathematics

What you need:

- Cardboard boxes in various sizes
- Tape
- Scissors
- Glue
- Circle compass
- Ruler
- Pencil
- Cutting mat
- Craft knife
- Adhesive contact paper
- Small balls

What to do:

1. Create some thin cardboard shapes such as circles, triangles and squares, using a compass and/or ruler and pencil, and scissors.

2. To make a giant shape sorter: carefully flatten a box and whilst it is flat, draw the desired shapes (matching those made in Step 1) on all six sides. Slide a cutting mat behind the shapes and cut them out using a craft knife (adult only) so that you are left with a box that has various shaped holes in it. Open the box out again.

3. If you have adhesive contact paper, cover the cardboard shapes with this to protect them and give them a bit of longevity! Seal the edges of the cardboard box shape-sorter using glue.

4. Give children the flat shapes and small balls to put through the holes of the shape sorter.

aking it forward

Try making 3D cardboard shapes using tape and glue.

bservation questions

Does the child know any shapes?

Can the child recognise patterns?

Does the child notice similarities and differences?

Vhat's in it for the children?

hildren will develop an increased iterest in representation and basic rrangements.

Floor puzzle

Mathematics

What you need:

- Cardboard boxes in various sizes
- Old poster
- Scissors
- Glue
- Black marker pens
- Craft knife

What to do:

1. Flatten a cardboard box and cut out a large rectangle.
2. Create a picture on the rectangular base board by drawing, painting or using decoupage or glue.
3. Mark the picture to divide it into puzzle pieces and cut these out with a craft knife (adult only).
4. Challenge the children to recreate the picture putting the puzzle pieces together.

Taking it forward

- Make individual puzzles (to take home).
- Use a group photograph on a puzzle.

Observation questions

- Does the child pay attention to detail?
- Does the child show interest in patterns?
- How long does the child concentrate?

What's in it for the children?

The activity will develop children's ability to pay attention to details and patterns, and it will promote logical thinking.

✚ Health & Safety

Warn children about the potential dangers of sharp implements and equipment.

Colour dice and colour matching

Mathematics

What you need:

- Square tissue box or other thin cardboard box
- Glue
- Paper in different colours
- Scissors

What to do:

1. If using a square tissue box, cover all side with glue and a different colour of paper on each of the faces.

2. Alternatively, use a template (like the one below) to make a cardboard cube. Fold the cube into shape and use the tabs to glue the box together.

3. Cover all sides of the cube with glue and a different coloured paper per face of the dice.

4. The dice can be used in circle time to encourage children to take turns rolling it and then finding matching coloured objects around the room.

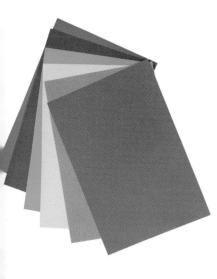

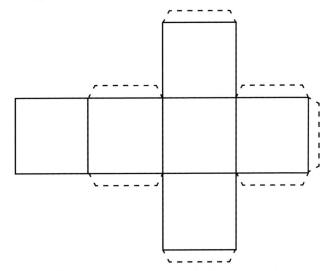

Taking it forward

- Children can roll the dice and organise a themed day, for example a Red Day.

Observation questions

- Does the child know their colours?
- Can the child recognise and match similar colours?

What's in it for the children?

Children will use descriptive language and notice characteristics of different colours.

Make your own coins

What you need:

- Variety of real coins
- Cardboard
- Pen
- Scissors
- Aluminium foil
- Flattening object, e.g. small bottle

What to do:

1. Place one of the real coins on a piece of cardboard and use a pen to carefully trace around it.

2. Cut out the coin shape from the cardboard using scissors.

3. Use a small piece of aluminium foil to cover the coin completely, dull side down and shiny side on top.

4. Smooth out the foil covering on the top side of the cardboard coin using your finger or any object that has a flat, hard surface, for example the bottom of a small bottle.

5. Use the real coin to make an impression on the cardboard coin by pressing it firmly into the foil.

Taking it forward

- Use silver and gold metallic paint instead of foil and draw in the detail on the top of each coin.
- Create notes to represent larger numbers/larger amounts of money.
- Use the money in role play, for example in a shop or paying for a bus ticket.

Observation questions

- Does the child know any numbers and/or numerals?
- Does the child show interest in role play including counting?

What's in it for the children?

Children will develop an ability to estimate, notice and recognise numerals linked to quantities.

Big book
Literacy

What you need:

- Cardboard boxes in various sizes
- Glue
- Scissors
- String or large brass fastener
- Masking tape
- Old newspapers and magazines

What to do:

1. Cut out cardboard pages and a cardboard cover to make a book.

2. Place the pages on top of each other and pierce two holes to secure them with string or brass fasteners and trim the edges.

3. Start layering tape across the spine of the book to bind it, and cover the entire spine with tape. Add tape in the other direction along the spine of the book.

4. Ask children to decorate the book. The book is the perfect medium to record group events, to make notes or to store collectables from journeys like leaves, sticks or feathers. Children can create their own magazine, decorated with cut out pictures and letters.

Taking it forward

- Make your own version of favourite or classic stories.

- Ask the children to each draw a page to create a group art book.

Observation questions

- Does the child cooperate?

- Does the child show an interest in print/books?

- Does the child use descriptive communication (verbal or non-verbal)?

What's in it for the children?

Children will develop an understanding of the connection between spoken language and print.

Story and drama boxes

Literacy

What you need:

- A large cardboard box
- Pictures from children's classic stories
- Fabric, scarves, old pieces of clothing, old hats, old shoes, gloves etc.
- Soft cardboard boxes in various sizes
- Newspaper or coloured paper
- Scissors
- Masking tape
- Glue

What to do:

1. Cut the flaps off a large cardboard box and decorate it with pictures of classic children's stories.

2. Collect fabric, scarves, old pieces of clothing, old hats, old shoes, gloves etc. to encourage the children to dress up and place these in the drama box made in step 1.

3. To make the storyteller's hat: draw a quarter circle on a large piece of thin, strong cardboard. For a child sized hat, make each of the straight sides at least 40cm long. Draw a line around the curved edge, about 2½cm from the edge. Mark even lines all the way around the curved edge to the line edge. Cut slits along each of the marked lines. These slits will be used as tabs, to attach the cone to the brim.

4. Putting the cone to one side, now draw a circle with a diameter of 37cm on another piece of cardboard. Draw an oval shape in the centre of this circle, leaving plenty of space all sides around. This will fit the head of the wearer. Cut out the edge circle, then the inner oval. Attach the brim to the hat. by rolling the quarter circle into a cone shape. Tape or staple the edges together, then fold out the tabs and to the underside of the brim. Continue until each tab has been attached, then decorate the hat if required.

5. To add elastic to keep the hat in place, pierce two small holes on either side of the brim, spaced evenly across from each other. Cut a length of elastic that will fit around the wearer's chin area comfortably (measure first), leaving extra for tying small knots.Once threaded through the holes, then cut off the excess. Add newspaper strips to the bottom of the hat for hair if desired.

6. Use the hats with the drama boxes to create a story telling corner and encourage the children to dress up to tell familiar stories.

aking it forward

Make separate drama boxes for particular stories, for example a Little Red Riding Hood box.

Make boxes suiting different cultures, using stories originating from different countries.

Add CDs and/or musical instruments to the drama boxes.

bservation questions

Does the child show interest in dressing up?

Can the child impersonate different characters?

Does the child use different sounds/tones to differentiate between characters?

hat's in it for the children?

hildren will learn to describe ain story setting, developing an nderstanding of different characters, mes, events.

Notepad

Literacy

What you need:

- Thin cardboard boxes in various sizes
- Coloured paper
- Scissors
- Binder clips
- Padding compound

What to do:

1. Take a stack of paper — any colour, type, or size.
2. Tap it on the table so that the pages are in a squared-off stack, ready for securing together.
3. For a sturdy cover, add a piece of cardboard, cut to the same size as the paper. Secure the sheets together with a couple of binder clips along the top.
4. Take a small brush and apply the padding compound liberally along the left-hand long edge of the pad and let it dry to a smooth and non-sticky finish (for a large notepad apply a second or third coat for extra strength). Once dry, remove the binder clips at the top of the notepad.
5. Children can make marks or write in their own notepad.

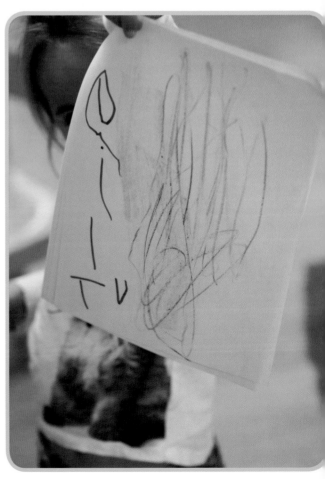

Taking it forward

- Organise an exhibition of the children's notpads.
- Make a group dictionary with simple words and pictures.

Observation questions

- Does the child show an interest in mark making?
- Does the child know or name any letters?

What's in it for the children?

Children will make marks, linking sounds and meaning to symbols, whilst developing hand strength to prepare for writing.

What you need:

- Thin cardboard boxes in various sizes
- Scissors
- Markers
- Masking tape

What to do:

1. Flatten a cardboard box.

2. Help the children to draw the letters of the alphabet in large sizes.

3. Cut around each letter and cover with masking tape to strengthen.

4. The collection of letters can be used in circle time to visualise the names of the children.

Taking it forward

- Use in games such as: all children get a letter and try to find objects starting with that letter.

Observation questions

- Can the child recognise similar sounds?

- Does the child know or name any letters?

What's in it for the children?

Children will experience linking sounds to letters and print, creating simple words.

Storyboard

Literacy

What you need:

- A large cardboard box
- Thin cardboard boxes in various sizes
- Knife
- Newspaper, magazines
- Scissors
- Glue
- Two-sided, self-adhesive Velcro tape
- Large piece of felt (optional)

Taking it forward

- Organise theatre and storytelling events.
- Ask children to create their own stories and act them out on the storyboard.

Observation questions

- Does the child show interest in storytelling?
- How expressive is the child's vocabulary?

What's in it for the children?

Children will start to handle print with personal interest.

 Health & Safety

Warn children about the potential dangers of sharp implements and equipment. Supervise them carefully when they are using these tools.

What to do:

1. Flatten a large cardboard box. Depending on the space given, your storyboard can be free standing or hanging. For a free standing board, make it sturdier by cutting out two large triangles from serrated, strong cardboard with a knife, then bend them lengthwise down the middle and glue around the two bottom corners to reinforce them..

2. Optionally, cover the board with felt fabric.

3. Cut the double-sided Velcro tape into small, 2cm pieces and secure one side onto the board, scattered around the storyboard.

4. Create small story characters and objects by drawing or cutting them out from newspapers or magazines. Glue them onto cardboard, cut them out then apply a piece of Velcro tape to the back of each.

5. Use the board in storytelling sessions, inviting children to stick their own characters on the board and move them about.

What you need:

- A large cardboard box
- Paint, paintbrush
- Scissors

What to do:

1. Paint a large box with bright red paint and let it dry.

2. Using a knife or scissors, cut out a rectangle at the top of the box that is large enough to fit A4 sized envelopes through.

3. Customise the postal collection box by writing the words 'Royal Mail,' 'Letter Box' or the name of your nursery or setting.

4. Use the post box for a variety of tasks, including creative writing and celebrating birthdays.

Taking it forward

Children can post letters to their favourite people.

Visit a real post office and/or invite a post person in to talk to the children.

Create the children's own post bag by securing an old tie strap onto a smaller box.

Observation questions

Does the child form letters?

How does the child use their hands to draw/cut/form marks?

What's in it for the children?

Children will make meaningful marks and begin to form letters.

Signs

Literacy

What you need:

- Thin cardboard boxes in various sizes
- Long cardboard tubes
- Black and metallic traffic light coloured card
- Scissors
- Markers
- Masking tape
- Coloured paper
- Glue

What to do:

1. To make traffic signs: wrap a cardboard paper tube in black card.

2. Trace around one end of the tube and cut out a circle of black card slightly larger than the circumference of the tube, then pierce a hole in the centre of the circle, attach some thread and secure with tape. Glue this circle and thread to one end of the tube.

3. Fold another piece of black card around the top of the tube to form a four sided box shape big enough to use as the traffic lights.

4. Cut three circles out from one side of the box, and save them as templates for Step 5. Then, stick the edges of the black card box shape together.

5. Use the circle template, saved from earlier, to cut out three squares of traffic light coloured metallic paper, slightly larger than the template. Line these up with the holes in the black card box shape, and glue the traffic light coloured paper at the appropriate levels.

6. Cut out another square of black card and pierce a small hole in the centre. Slide the tube into the box from Step 5, and poke the thread from Step 2 through the new square of card. Glue the square to the black card traffic light box to bind the top of the traffic lights to the tube, making sure that the tube can still move and turn freely and the thread is still coming out the top.

7. Encourage the children to use the traffic lights in their role play outdoors when on scooters, bikes and in mini cars.

aking it forward

Make a large standing triangular sign to remind children of the rules of the room (for example, pictures to indicate the use of kind hands, kind mouth and kind feet).

Make signs to mark the areas of the room.

bservation questions

Does the child understand that the picture or words have a meaning that can be said?

Does the child link marks to meaning?

Does the child use their own signs and marks to convey meaning?

hat's in it for the children?

hildren will distinguish between ifferent marks and understand that ymbols carry meaning.

Cardboard canvas

Creative, imaginative and expressive development

What you need:

- Cardboard boxes
- PVA glue
- Masking tape
- Brush
- Pages from an unwanted book, or tissue paper

What to do:

1. Cut up the cardboard boxes along all edges. The lid flaps make excellent smaller canvases.

2. Increase the thickness by using more layers of cardboard. Use masking tape and tape them horizontally and vertically.

3. Apply glue to your canvas and collage book pages on it (optionally add tissue paper for a textured effect). Let it dry then it is ready for children to paint or collage on it.

Taking it forward

- Organise an exhibition.
- Sell children's artwork to raise funds for a chosen charity.

Observation questions

- Does the child use different types of media to express themselves?

What's in it for the children?

Children will make marks and manipulate material to personalise their environment.

Cardboard paper

Creative, imaginative and expressive development

What you need:

- Small pieces of scrap cardboard and paper
- Cornstarch (optional)
- Blender
- Rolling pin
- Sponge
- Cardboard for drying
- Wooden frame, wire mesh staples or wires
- Extra ingredients like dried herbs, leaves, flowers, seeds, spices etc.

What to do:

1. Collect clean cardboard and newspaper scraps.

2. Tear all the gathered scrap paper and cardboard into small pieces then soak overnight in a vat of water (two parts water to one part paper). A tablespoon of cornstarch will accelerate the dissolving process, but is not necessary.

3. Mix the wet paper and water in a blender until it reaches the consistency of gravy.

4. Make a screen frame by attaching a wire mesh to a wooden frame with staples or wires.

5. Place the screen in the large bowl and then slowly pour the pulp onto the frame, adding extra ingredients like the dried herbs at this point. Try to make sure the pulp is evenly spread on the screen.

6. Press out the water that remains in the pulp on the screen using a rolling pin. Be sure to squeeze as much water out as possible.

7. Carefully turn the screen over and tap the recycled paper onto a piece of flat cardboard. Press the recycled paper flat, and let it dry for 24 hours. Then peel it off the newspaper and trim to the desired shape for notepads, cards etc.

Taking it forward

Make personalised birthday cards.

Observation questions

Does the child get involved in the activity?

Does the child ask questions and show interest?

What's in it for the children?

Children will study different types of media, whilst also learning about sustainability.

fantastic things to do with cardboard

Mirror blocks
Creative, imaginative and expressive development

What you need:

- Small square cardboard boxes, such as tissue box
- Glue
- Reflective materials such as foil

What to do:

1. Collect materials.

2. Cut the reflective material to fit the size of the box (a piece to cover each of the four sides).

3. Cover the box with glue and secure the pieces of reflective material. Leave it to dry.

4. Encourage the children to use the mirror blocks in circle time to explore their own features, movements, body parts etc.

Taking it forward

- Copy various facial expressions.
- Look through magazines and let the children compare their own features to those of others, to develop descriptive vocabulary.

Observation questions

- Can the child use descriptive language?
- Can the child manipulate their own face/body to imitate or express?

What's in it for the children?

Children will develop an interest in different ways to express themselves.

Natural paints for cardboard

Creative, imaginative and expressive development

What you need:

Natural materials such as:

- **Brown** – natural soil or earth
- **Purple/pink/red/lilac/ blue** – berries, or beetroot, blackberries, blueberries, elderberries, blackcurrants, redcurrants, bilberries, raspberries, strawberries etc.
- **Red/orange** – paprika, chilli powder, powder of broken terracotta pots
- **Black** – soot or charcoal
- **Grey** – wood ash (or mix charcoal and chalk)
- **White** – chalk or talcum powder
- **Yellow** – crab apples if available or turmeric which gives a beautiful golden yellow
- **Green** – spinach, herbs

What to do:

1. Collect the colourful natural materials.
2. Prepare small bowls or egg cartons and mash or grate ingredients, or for a finer finish use a blender.
3. Mix ingredients with water, pour into bowls according to colour, and start painting on cardboard.

Taking it forward

- Make themed colour days.
- Children can do face painting/make up (for fun or for drama) – need to be cautious of allergies.

Observational questions

- Does the child respond to different materials? How?

What's in it for the children?

Children will explore different textures and materials, whilst learning about sustainability.

Health & Safety

Be aware of any allergies when handling these materials.

Cardboard band

Creative, imaginative and expressive development

What you need:

- Selection of cardboard boxes
- Duct tape or masking tape
- Wooden sticks
- Cardboard tubes in different sizes
- Thin plywood
- Rattling material like pebbles or beads
- Heavy-duty foil or pieces of old fabric
- Scissors

What to do:

1. Arrange a selection of cardboard boxes around a chair and tape it together with duct tape or masking tape for an instant drum set.

2. For a twirling drum/shaker glue two paper plates together or use a cardboard tube. Attach the plates or tube to a stick, and thread two beads onto a string, then attach the top of the string to the top of the cardboard shaker, so when rotating the beads flip-flop against it to make the sound.

3. Use different sized cardboard tubes of different lengths and thicknesses as 'boomwhackers' to bang against different surfaces.

4. To make a simple drum glue a thin piece of plywood securely over a length of wide tubing (or a tube created from gluing a rectangular piece of serrated cardboard). Make bongo drums by fastening short tubes of contrasting lengths together.

5. Create rattles or rainsticks by placing a quantity of different rattling materials inside a long tube and securing the ends with heavy-duty foil or pieces of fabric and rubber bands.

Taking it forward

Create a band and organise a concert.

Listen to different types of music from different eras and cultures, notice the similarities and differences and try to copy.

Observation questions

Does the child show an interest in rhythm or in expressing with rhythms?

Does the child notice patterns of music?

What's in it for the children?

Children will enjoy sounds and develop an understanding of the elements of music.

The gallery

Creative, imaginative and expressive development

What you need:

- Selection of large cardboard boxes
- Scissors
- Glue and tape
- Children's artwork

What to do:

1. Arrange a selection of cardboard boxes (ideally one for each child in the group) into a pyramid by standing the boxes on their sides with the open side facing out.

2. Once you are satisfied with the arrangement, cut the top off each box, then recreate the pyramid and secure it with glue and tape.

3. Use the individual sections as a holding bay for the children's artwork and display it as a free-standing, unique gallery.

Taking it forward

- Organise an exhibition evening for families and friends.

Observation questions

- Does the child appreciate the ownership of individual space? How?

- Does the child express a sense of pride?

- Does the child show interest in the work of others?

What's in it for the children?

Children will construct with a purpose in mind, to gain an understanding of the means of individual expression.

The mixing pots

Creative, imaginative and expressive development

What you need:

- Selection of small cardboard boxes or egg cartons
- Powder paint in a variety of colours
- Textured ingredients such as flour, sand, gravel stones, herbs, glitter etc.

What to do:

1. Cut the top flaps off a selection of cardboard boxes and arrange these cardboard flaps in front of the children.

2. Supply powder paint in different colours and allow the children to mix the colours on their cardboard palettes (or you may wish to use egg cartons).

3. Add different textured ingredients to achieve textured paint and create pictures on the sides of the boxes.

Taking it forward

Use the textured paint on old T-shirts and organise a fashion show.

Observation questions

How does the child manipulate materials: do they use hands or tools?

How does the child react when encountering new experiences?

What's in it for the children?

Children will developing an understanding of materials, characteristics of materials (such as colour, texture etc.) and will gain experience in manipulation and creation.

Health & Safety

Remind children not to insert small items such as gravel in their mouths or noses.

50 fantastic things to do with cardboard

Tearoom

Understanding the world

What you need:

- Very large cardboard box such as furniture box
- Fairy lights and cable ties (optional)
- Small sturdy boxes and masking tape
- Pillows and table cloth
- Teaset

What to do:

1. Cut the top flaps off a large cardboard box and stand upright.

2. Optionally fix fairy lights around the box (your 'table') using cable ties.

3. Strengthen some small boxes with masking tape and stand upright to create stools to fit round the table. Add pillows and tablecloths for a stylish touch.

4. Place a teaset on the top of table and encourage children to role play.

Taking it forward

- Create cardboard menus and money to use for role play.

- Use real tea and cakes and organise themed days to taste food from different cultures.

Observation questions

- Does the child express their views of others?

- Does the child show interest in different cultures?

What's in it for the children?

Children will share information about the lives of themselves and others. They will practise social interaction and experience social rules of acceptance.

Surprise boxes for harvest

Understanding the world

What you need:

- Empty shoeboxes
- Children's artwork
- Glue
- Decorating materials
- Ribbons
- Collected small food items such as cans of fruit, small jam jars, bags of nuts, small biscuit packets etc.

What to do:

1. Decorate the shoeboxes with children's artwork.
2. Place a selection of the food items into each shoebox.
3. Tie a decorative ribbon around the box.
4. Visit local communities (such as homes for the elderly, children centres) to hand out the surprise boxes as harvest gifts.

Taking it forward

Make surprise boxes for Christmas and use to take gifts to a local hospital.

Observation questions

How does the child relate to the act of giving?

What's in it for the children?

Children will create positive links with local communities, while also learning about their own surroundings and their immediate society.

fantastic things to do with cardboard

Festival boxes
Understanding the world

What you need:

- A large cardboard box
- Thin cardboard boxes in various sizes
- Scissors
- Masking tape
- Glue
- Fabric, scarves, hats, shoes to represent different cultures (for example Chinese silk, Indian scarves, Mexican hats)
- Face paint
- Musical instruments from different cultures
- Plant pot
- Feathers

What to do:

1. Cut the top off a large cardboard box and decorate it with pictures of people from different cultures.

2. Collect fabric, scarves, old pieces of clothing, old hats, old shoes, gloves, face paint and native musical instruments to encourage the children to dress up. Put them in your themed festival boxes.

3. Create dressing up accessories from cardboard, as follows.

To make a Mexican hat: Wrap a piece of card around a plant pot and cut accordingly – this is the upper part of your hat. Place the hat on top of a large piece of thick construction paper to create the brim: trace a large circle and cut neatly along the edge. Cut out an inner circle large enough to fit head. Glue the top of the hat and the brim together. Paint the hat a solid colour. Let it dry. Hide the glue line, where the two pieces were attached, by gluing a row of coloured pom-poms or other adornments. Decorate the rest of the sombrero with crayons, cut outs and other embellishments. Poke a hole on either side of the fitted piece of the hat. Attach a string through each hole securing it in place by knotting each end or attach a large bead to each side. Tie the two ends together. Add trim along the edge of the sombrero.

To make a tribal headdress: Measure a long strip of corrugated cardboard around the front to the back of the child's head. Hold the strip so it fits snugly on the child's head and snip off any excess. Lay the cardboard band flat and cover with a piece of wide ribbon, leaving at least 15 cm of ribbon extending on each end of the cardboard to be used as tails at the back of the headdress. Attach the ribbon to the cardboard with glue. Apply feathers (real or cardboard cut outs) and arrange them in a row with the longest feathers in the centre, and secure it with glue. Roll the piece of cardboard around into a circle and attach the ends of the cardboard together with a line of glue. Allow the ribbon ends to dangle at the back of the headdress.

Taking it forward

Make separate boxes for different cultures and fill with cardboard items, such as Diwali lanterns.

Observation questions

Does the child show interest in different cultures?

What's in it for the children?

Children will learn about different traditions, customs and communities, whilst encouraging communication and social connections.

A touchy-feely box

Understanding the world

What you need:

- Empty shoeboxes
- Children's artwork
- Glue
- Decorating materials
- Small items to represent children's environment such as leaves, sticks, objects

What to do:

1. Decorate the shoeboxes with children's pictures.

2. Cut a hole on the top of the box, big enough for children to push their hands through.

3. Fill the box with objects.

4. Use the boxes in circle time, by asking children to pull out an object and try to describe where they have seen it in their surroundings. Create a discussion among the children inviting others to join in.

Taking it forward

- Make a separate box for different part of the environment for example garden, bathroom, dining room, etc.

Observation questions

- Does the child recognise the object?
- Does the child use descriptive language?

What's in it for the children?

Children will develop a greater ability to pay attention to detail and to notice the environment.

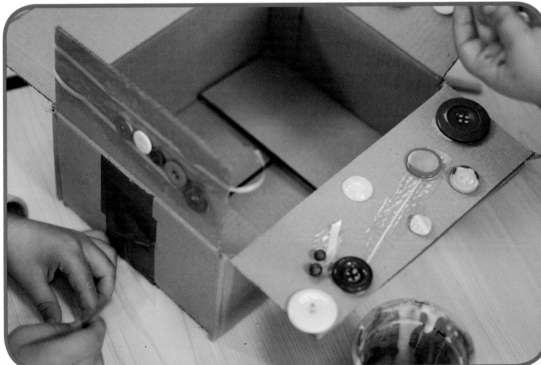

I-spy binoculars
Understanding the world

What you need:

- Empty toilet paper rolls
- Thin cardboard
- Scissors
- Tape
- Plastic wrap
- PVA glue
- Rubber bands
- Coloured paper
- Hole punch
- Ribbon, yarn or string
- Markers or crayons
- Stickers

What to do:

1. Cut two empty paper rolls to exactly the same length or use soft cardboard instead. Cut one piece of construction paper width wise. Roll each cut piece into a tube, and tape it in place. Make sure they are exactly the same size.

2. Cut two small pieces of plastic wrap just large enough to cover one end of each tube.

3. Apply a small amount of glue around the outside of each tube approximately 2cm from the end. Whilst the glue is still wet, place one square of plastic wrap on each tube so that it covers the circular opening on one end and adheres to the glue. Place a rubber band around the plastic wrap to hold it in place whilst the glue dries.

4. Use craft glue to glue the two tubes together so they sit side by side, with the plastic-wrapped ends on the same side. Secure the tubes together by placing rubber bands around them or use double-sided tape.

5. Cover the tubes with coloured paper, leaving the ends free.

6. Punch a hole on the outside of each of the tubes, close to the end that does not have the plastic wrap. Tie a piece of ribbon, yarn or string through the holes to make a neck strap for the binoculars.

Taking it forward

Go on a forest journey and use the binoculars to watch birds.

Observation questions

Does the child notice things?

Does the child use descriptive language?

What's in it for the children?

Children will use their experience to extend their knowledge about the surrounding world.

The family car
Understanding the world

What you need:

- Cardboard boxes
- Paper cups
- Paper plates
- Sticks
- Glue
- Scissors and knife
- Fabric
- Skewers
- Markers, crayons, stickers

What to do:

1. To make big car: seal a large cardboard box with tape. Trace two doors in the two longer sides. The semi-circle lines should begin at the halfway point lengthwise and drop down, so their flat side is along the top of the box. Cut out the doors.

To make the windshield, cut along the top edges of the box, about two thirds of the way around. Start just in front of one door and continue moving back towards the rear, then finally along the other side. Don't cut the piece out entirely – leave this flap attached to the hood (the top front third). Lift the flap and fold it halfway down, towards the interior of the car. Tape the top fold to the bottom half to secure the windshield. Cut a large rectangle out of the folded section to make a window on it.

Cut a portion of the back and fold it down forming the seats.

Glue two cups to the front of the car so that their base is attached and the wider lip faces out, to form the headlights. Add details on the car, like adding sticks to form the grill. Glue two paper plates along the length of each side for wheels.

Create an interior by glueing in fabric for upholstery, and add another paper plate to the 'dashboard' as the steering wheel. Paint and decorate the car.

2. To make small car: start with a small cardboard box. Make an incision around the sides and over the top. Start about 10 cm from the front of the car and 7 cm below the top. Cut upwards to the top, across the top, and 7 cm down the other side. Fold down the front section (the one just been cut around).

Shape the rear of the car as an old-fashioned design. Pierce the sides at the points where the wheels should go with the sharp end of the scissors. Insert two skewer for axles, running between the two sets of pierced points. Cut four wheels of equal diameter out of another piece of stiffer cardboard. Attach the wheels to the axels, poking a hole in the wheel with the sharp end of skewers. Decorate the car with markers, crayons and stickers.

aking it forward

Make large car for children to sit in, encouraging role play.

Make other vehicles such as aeroplane, bus or a boat.

Make traffic lights, shop, petrol station to create a city/street scene with traffic.

bservation questions

Does the child talk about own experiences?

Does the child distinguish between past and present?

hat's in it for the children?

hildren will investigate means of avel in the changing world, learning to anipulate the environment.

✚ Health & Safety

Warn children about the potential dangers of sharp implements and equipment. Supervise them carefully when they are using these tools.

) fantastic things to do with cardboard

Mini garden
Understanding the world

What you need:

- **Planting soil**
- **Seeds** (herbs are ideal)
- **Gravel stone**
- **Empty egg cartons** (plastic or paper)
- **Empty milk cartons**

What to do:

1. Use empty egg cartons or milk cartons.

2. Cut the lid off an egg carton with scissors or a sharp knife, or cut the top off a milk carton, and set aside.

3. Poke a small drainage hole in the bottom of each egg cell using the tip of a pencil or similar object. Place the egg or milk carton lid under the bottom to create a drainage tray. Fill the egg cells or milk carton half to three-quarters full with potting mixture or with a mixture of soil and gravel stones (avoid regular garden soil, which is too heavy and soon becomes compacted, preventing free circulation of air and water through the soil).

4. Plant two or three seeds on top of the potting mixture in each cell. Cover the seeds with a thin layer of potting mixture. Refer to the seed packet for specific depth requirements.

5. Water the potting mixture lightly with a spray bottle. Mist as needed to keep the potting mixture lightly moist.

6. Keep an eye out as the seeds grow, and plant out if needed.

Taking it forward

- Organise a growing competition.
- Visit the local farmers' market.

Observation questions

- Does the child show interest in unique activities like gardening?
- Does the child link everyday activities to new experiences? How?

What's in it for the children?

Children will make connection with the natural world, and gain a better understanding of where people come from.